HOW SHOULD I
**EXERCISE
HOSPITALITY?**

CULTIVATING BIBLICAL GODLINESS

Series Editors
Joel R. Beeke and Ryan M. McGraw

Dr. D. Martyn Lloyd-Jones once said that what the church needs to do most of all is "to begin herself to live the Christian life. If she did that, men and women would be crowding into our buildings. They would say, 'What is the secret of this?'" As Christians, one of our greatest needs is for the Spirit of God to cultivate biblical godliness in us in order to put the beauty of Christ on display through us, all to the glory of the triune God. With this goal in mind, this series of booklets treats matters vital to Christian experience at a basic level. Each booklet addresses a specific question in order to inform the mind, warm the affections, and transform the whole person by the Spirit's grace, so that the church may adorn the doctrine of God our Savior in all things.

HOW SHOULD I
EXERCISE
HOSPITALITY?

REBECCA VANDOODEWAARD

REFORMATION HERITAGE BOOKS
GRAND RAPIDS, MICHIGAN

Reformation Heritage Books
2965 Leonard St. NE
Grand Rapids, MI 49525
616-977-0889 / Fax 616-285-3246
orders@heritagebooks.org
www.heritagebooks.org

Printed in the United States of America
17 18 19 20 21 22/10 9 8 7 6 5 4 3 2 1

ISBN 978-1-60178-547-3

For additional Reformed literature, request a free book list from Reformation Heritage Books at the above regular or e-mail address.

HOW SHOULD I
EXERCISE HOSPITALITY?

———✗———

While my husband and I were living overseas, an older couple in the church invited us over for Sunday lunch. We were excited; not only did we have no friends in the whole country, but we also had no car, and walking everywhere had given us massive appetites. The dining table was beautifully set with china and silver, each course was delicious, and our hosts guided the conversation for several pleasant hours. But it was not only one lunch; they frequently invited us over for meals during our months there, opening their home to us and caring for us so well. We appreciated the food—the hostess was a wonderful cook—but even more we loved the fellowship, learning a lot about conversation and Christian love from this couple.

You might be tempted, as I was, to explain this talent away: "Clearly, the hostess had the gift of hospitality." She certainly was gifted at it, but that is not because hospitality is a spiritual gift given to a portion of the Christian population. In the New

Testament lists of spiritual gifts, hospitality is not one of them. The closest thing we have in those passages is the gift of serving (Rom. 12:6–8; 1 Peter 4:11), and it is a different word than the one for hospitality. Hospitality is not a gift. It is a command (Rom. 12:13).

In other words, hospitality does not fall into the category of, "If I'm good at it or have time for it or if I want to, then I'll do it." It is not like playing the piano for church or volunteering for the building committee or organizing a retreat. Practicing hospitality is in the same category as loving: something all Christians are supposed to do regardless of their inclinations, gifts, wealth, social status, or past experience. If we are not practicing hospitality, we are disobeying. Why is this such a big deal? Hospitality is serious because of who God is and what He has done.

You may know that hospitality literally translates as a "love of strangers" (Heb. 13:2). It is us reaching out to people whom we do not know and opening our homes and lives to them. Fellowship is having friends and family over for visits. Everybody does that. Hospitality is having strangers over to serve them, especially strangers who cannot return the deed. Christians do that. Christians must do it because it is a reflection of God's character and the gospel.

Before creation, the Trinity existed in perfect communion and fellowship among the persons. There was no lack, no need, no emptiness. But God still chose to make man, and not only to make him, but as we read further into Genesis and then the rest of Scripture, we learn that God redeems strangers to grace, bringing them into union with Christ. Enemies have become fellow heirs (Eph. 2:6). God welcomes us into the family, into holy fellowship, at immeasurable cost to Himself.

But that is not all. What does Christ tell the disciples in John 14? That He is going to prepare a place for them (v. 3). And it is not some impersonal place, like a restaurant or coffee shop, where people can meet before going their separate ways. The place Christ is preparing for His people is the Father's house (v. 2).

This should astound us. Salvation is divine hospitality to strangers—to us. From Genesis to Revelation and into eternity, God shows hospitality to former enemies. This gives perspective to the command, doesn't it? Hospitality is not just something we do. If we are Christians, it is an act that reflects the reality of salvation.

But this should not just astound us. If we really understand it, it will transform the way we live. We will start practicing hospitality! Hospitality does not require fine china, multiple courses, or perfectly clean and decorated homes. It requires that we share our time, homes, meals, and fellowship with others—and if we understand salvation, we will want to do so. Thinking through the practical issues of inviting people into our homes can make practicing it easier. Here are seven ways that can help us think practically about how to follow our Lord's command in this area.

PRACTICE HOSPITALITY PROMISCUOUSLY

The ninth chapter of Proverbs gives us an interesting scene. A woman, Wisdom, is building a house with a dining room. She has even carved pillars for it. She has butchered cows that she has raised, selected some good wine to go with the beef, and set the table nicely. While she finishes preparing, she tells her maids to go out and let the guests know that dinner is served. Who is she inviting? Everyone. Her maids are going through the streets calling to everyone who is simple, everyone who lacks sense. That is all of us by nature. We are all invited.

We do not need to drive through town with a loudspeaker, letting everyone know that supper will be at 6:00 at our place. That is not the point of the passage. The point is that salvation is open and free to all who will come. As believers, our hospitality should reflect the same kind of love and openness that God has for the world (John 3:16). We do not have the capacity to host at the same time all who will come; we are mortal. But we can reflect this heavenly capacity bit by bit by opening our homes at different times to all kinds of people. When Jesus told the disciples to go into all nations, preaching the good news of salvation, He did not place any limits on that proclamation. It was to every kind and class and type of person (Matt. 28:19). Hospitality should have the same indiscriminate, promiscuous vision. Are we placing limits on the kinds of people we have into our homes?

Do we invite people of different ages? This can be hard on a practical level. A retired couple hosting a young family might realize that their home is not as toddler-proof as they thought it was. A family with teenagers might find that they need to grow in thoughtfulness for the elderly or in patience with fussy babies. It is relatively easy to host people in the same stage of life that we are, but it places artificial limits on hospitality that stratifies God's children by age. That is not healthy.

Do we have people of different ethnicities in our homes? Maybe we live in northeast Montana, and there just is not anyone of a different ethnicity for hundreds of miles. Clearly, circumstances play into this. But most of us live in or near cities, and most cities are multiethnic. Does your guest list reflect the ethnic diversity of your community? If not, why?

How about backgrounds? Are you afraid to invite the teacher and her family because you never went to college and are afraid of what you would talk about? Do you stay away from inviting believers from other denominations because you do not think that they are entirely orthodox? How about people from other cultures? Do you stick with people from your own background so that you do not have to deal with the awkwardness of language and cultural barriers?

What about circumstances or gifts? Have you chosen not to invite the older woman who is a great cook because you know you are not? Do you think the unbelieving neighbor could never come over because they know you're a Christian and heard you shout at your kids in the backyard? What about the wealthy couple at church? Do we stay away from asking them because we are afraid of what they will think of our house, or we will not be able to feed them like they are used to?

I have. But these—and all other excuses for limiting hospitality to our comfort zone—are pride, laziness, or both.

Preachers are taught to think about the different categories in their congregation so that they can preach to all categories of people. We need to do the same when we think of whom to have into our homes. Singles, families, widowed, rich, poor, educated, ignorant, clean, messy, every age and every race—all should be welcome.

PRACTICE HOSPITALITY REGULARLY

Our hospitality needs to be regular. We cannot be given to hospitality (Rom. 12:13) if we have someone over only every month or so, or only in the summer, or only when the mood strikes us. Hospitality needs to be part of the fabric of our lifestyle, not a special occasion.

This rarely happens last minute; we have to plan for it and book time off. For our family, Sunday afternoons and Friday evenings are fairly predictable hospitality times, which means that we can slot in new folks from church, people we have just met at work, or unbelieving neighbors into the next available time. Creating regular times to have people in our homes not only helps us plan but also makes hospitality part of our regular routine. Once something is part of the routine, once something has a time slot, it becomes habit. The more often we do it, the less time it will take. It is better to do it more often, if possible, than less.

Do it at a time that works for your family; make visits suit your schedule. Think about the regular free time your family already has—the times when you go for a walk or have a barbeque or kick a ball around in the park—and use some of these times to practice hospitality. They are already set off from work, school, and church activities, so the time is there. All you have to do is add a few people and a bigger salad. This does not mean that every time you have an evening off you must invite people over, but it does mean that time off is a good opportunity to obey God's command.

Sundays are wonderful times to open your home to people. The Lord's Day is already set apart from work and framed by worship. Starting to work toward this on Monday will make it possible for your home to be a safe, refreshing place for other Christians on the Lord's Day. It is amazing how Satan uses Sundays to isolate and discourage God's people: new folks keenly feel the lack of friendships; students are tempted to catch up on homework; mothers can be frustrated with entertaining wired children through a long afternoon; singles can be very lonely leaving a full sanctuary and returning to an empty apartment. Sunday afternoons are a great tool not only for reaching strangers but also for building up brothers and sisters. They can be times of spiritual rest, emotional rejuvenation, and relational growth. In other words, Sunday hospitality can be a foretaste of celestial fellowship—worshipping and feasting together. It can reflect the eternal rest of heaven.

There are certain seasons of life that can limit hospitality for a time. Pregnancy, moving, sickness, and more can all be things that keep us from showing hospitality like we normally would. That is not neglecting the Lord's command; it is being wise in a particular season. But most of the time, we need to make hospitality part of the normal routine.

PRACTICE HOSPITALITY THOUGHTFULLY

When I think of having people over, the first things that I want to do are cook and clean. But there are other ways to prepare that we can easily neglect when we are getting ready for guests.

While we are chopping vegetables or vacuuming, we need to be thinking of the visit and planning for the conversation. What sort of person is coming over? What questions can we ask them to stimulate conversation when it dies down? Are there topics or headlines that we know they will want to discuss? Is there anything that would offend them that we need to avoid? My very hospitable father once ran outside during a meal and shot a stray cat in front of the dining room window, bringing a guest to tears. Try to avoid stuff like that.

Is there anything going on in their lives you should specifically ask about? If they are believers, how can you encourage them in Christ? If they are unbelievers, how can you share the gospel with them? Do you need to explain what you are doing in family worship? Run your thoughts by your spouse so that you can tag team during the visit.

What about any children who are coming over? Do you need to get out a basket of toys for a toddler or a board game for some teenagers? Is there a way to involve the children in the conversation?

If you are inviting more than one family or individual, you will also need to think about how they will interact and how you can help them enjoy each other's company. My mother once invited over two wonderful Christian families but did not think about the men's theological convictions; two male guests ended up on their feet, shouting at each other at the dinner table. It is something that has made both of us more thoughtful!

This thoughtfulness does not just have to avoid negative interaction, though. One older couple invited our family over as well as a family with children the same ages as ours so that everyone had someone to play with for the evening. Because of their thoughtfulness, the children had fun, and thus the adults could have a conversation!

Thinking through all these sorts of things can be a bit of work, but it will make the visit go smoothly and help your guests be more comfortable in your home.

PRACTICE HOSPITALITY CREATIVELY

Usually, hospitality will mean having people into our home and sharing food with them. This is the best way for people to get to know us and often the best way that we can serve. But it is not always possible. Sometimes, things happen in our lives that stop us from having people over. If a kitchen is in the middle of a renovation, throwing a dinner party is not going to go well. If we are caring for an elderly parent, inviting six young moms over for a playdate might not be loving. And sometimes there are situations where people will not be able to come to our homes for a meal. Perhaps a widow has trouble with mobility, or someone new to the country does not have a driver's license. Generally, most people will be able to come, but if there is a situation that prevents that, there are still many ways to practice hospitality.

We can bring meals to others. People often do this after someone has a baby, but that is usually dropping something off. Take a meal to a widower, eat it with him, do the clean-up, and visit for a bit afterward.

Perhaps someone is new to the area and is feeling hesitant about exploring. Pack a picnic and take them out to see something—the zoo, a park, or a museum.

Maybe there is a family that you are not comfortable having in your home and prefer to get to know them better first for some reason. Or maybe living in a small apartment makes it impractical to host a family for a meal. Take them and their kids to the park—pack water and snacks for everyone.

Sometimes a hectic time in a family schedule means that there just is not the time to clean the house and make a meal and have everyone eat it in the same two-hour window. Some seasons are like that. Meet another family for ice cream or a short hike.

The meal-at-a-table model of hospitality is the ideal one, but it is not always possible. It does not mean you cannot practice hospitality. It just means you get to try alternate ways of doing it until things can be brought back to normal again.

There are also situations where creativity means thinking outside the box in a different way. Is there a single mom in your church who just cannot find the time and space to have a birthday party for her son? Host one. Is there a widower who feels like he does not have the skills to have a family over? Ask him who he would like to get to know and invite everyone for brunch. We can also use hospitality to introduce old friends to new ones. Inviting a young couple from your congregation to meet a young couple that just moved in down the street can be a good way of connecting people and providing opportunities for friendships.

Another aspect of creativity is involving your children in hosting. Planning for them to help set the table, watch for arriving guests, open doors, entertain other children, help with younger children, and other jobs can not only teach them how to be hospitable, but teach them to love it. How can you involve your children—whatever their ages—in developing the skill of hospitality?

There are all sorts of ways to practice hospitality. Just make sure that your home and heart are open to people that need them.

PRACTICE HOSPITALITY PRAYERFULLY

If we believe that we need God's help and blessing to minister to others, then it would be foolish to practice hospitality without asking for it.

We need God's help not to be selfish. Hospitality is a lot of work, and we can begrudge the time and effort spent on our guests that we could have spent on ourselves. Money can be a factor, too. Proverbs 23:7 gives us a picture of a host telling his guests to eat up and enjoy the food while he figures out how much it is costing him. We can pray that God will give us a selflessness that loves to serve because we love Jesus.

We need God's help to love our guests. Some people are easy to love. They are thankful, helpful, and cheerful. Some people are not easy to love. They have attitudes, contrary opinions, and unappetizing manners. But the Lord does not tell us to love only people who are lovable. We are to love everyone, in humility, gentleness, and patience (Eph. 4:2). We can feed people an amazing meal and lead dazzling conversation, but if there is no love, we have not given them anything (1 Cor. 13:1–3). Most of us need to ask God to give us a Christlike love for people around us, regardless of how hard that loving will be.

We need God's blessing, or our work will be empty. I know people who do so much good. They work tirelessly for refugees or political change or nonprofits. They do it because they love people and sometimes because they are trying to outweigh some wrong they have done or evil that they see in the world. I have a lot to learn from them. But we can pour ourselves out day after day after day in a love that is disconnected from Christ, and all that work will end at our deaths. It will help people have more physical comfort or voice or justice in this world, and that is good. But it will not do anything for eternity. It will burn up with this world because it does not have God's blessing. Work done without this blessing, work that does not flow out of a heart that loves Christ and others, is lawlessness (Matt. 7:21–23). It might look like "mighty works," but it is hollow. That is a serious warning! But Scripture also gives us great encouragement. Matthew 10 tells us that even a cup of cold water given for Christ's sake brings blessing. That leaves us without guilt for our "ordinary" service and also brings comfort. The Lord sees and knows when we love Him. Amazingly, He also rewards it. Let's pray that promise back to Him when we have people coming over.

We can also pray specifically for our guests. If we know of a particular need or situation, we can be praying about it before they come. This is especially true if our guests are strangers to grace. Pray that the Lord would use this hospitality as a setting where they can taste and see that the Lord is good—perhaps especially during family worship. Having guests on your radar is a great reminder to bring them before the throne of grace! We can pray for specific ways to bless them during the visit.

And always, we can ask the Lord to use our feeble, bumbling means to produce spiritual growth in the souls gathered around our tables. He loves to answer prayer.

PRACTICE HOSPITALITY SACRIFICIALLY

Usually, when we invite people over, we expect to put some work into it but get a nice meal and a friendly visit out of it. Sometimes, that is what happens. But other times, visiting children reject your food and mess up the entire house; believers are critical of the church or other believers; unbelieving guests use crude language; some visitors may pocket your silver spoons (it happened to a friend). Our work, our emotional investment, our hopes for the visit or relationship, and sometimes our physical stuff gets sacrificed.

When things like this happen, we feel somehow cheated; our hospitality did not make us feel the way that we wanted it to. But when guests leave and we feel cheated or down, it is almost always because our hearts were not right before God when the guests walked in the door. Jonathan Goforth, the Canadian missionary to China, had this motto: "Seek to give much; expect nothing in return." And that is how we need to practice hospitality. God has given us everything, including our guests, and if the visit does not bless us, then it will sanctify us. Feeling that all that work was wasted on people who do not deserve it or appreciate it reveals that my heart was not ready to serve unconditionally, as the Lord calls me to. I was not ready to sacrifice that time, that energy, that food, and get nothing in return.

Preparing our hearts for sacrifice enables us to practice hospitality for Jesus's sake—to love our guests because Christ loved us first, to minister to them because the people who are least appealing are often the ones who most need gospel care. This kind of sacrificial hospitality might leave us tired and emotionally worn at the end of an evening (you might even be missing a few silver spoons), but it is the kind of hospitality that will not be consumed with the straw and stubble of this world—it is the kind of hospitality that God values and rewards because it is Spirit-enabled and Christlike. Our guests may never realize there was a sacrifice. They may not care. The Lord does. Expect to sacrifice, and remember what Christ sacrificed to welcome you.

PRACTICE HOSPITALITY EXPECTANTLY

There are sacrifices that come with hospitality. That is certain. But there are also blessings that we can expect when we obey the command to do it. What do you expect to get from hospitality? A good meal after a day of cleaning the house? A stimulating discussion? The opportunity to meet new people? All these things are part of the blessing of hospitality, but they are not all. There are blessings—spiritual and otherwise—that we experience here and now as we practice hospitality. God does not make it all sacrifice now and keep the blessing for when we get to eternity. In fact, we can expect a lot more than sacrifice when we obey this command.

Hebrews 13 gives us encouragement to practice hospitality by reminding us that Abraham welcomed strangers who ended up being angels (v. 2). In his commentary on Hebrews, John Calvin said that we can be tempted to think, "That was Abraham. That does not happen anymore." He points out that we should remember that we receive Christ Himself when we welcome the poor in His name (Mark 9:37).[1] Several times we have invited people

---

1. John Calvin, *Commentaries on the Epistle of Paul the Apostle to the Hebrews*, ed. and trans. John Owen (Grand Rapids: Baker, 1981), 340.

into our home knowing very little about them and have been remarkably blessed to have them. It often happens when we are the most tired or discouraged. God brings people right into our home to minister to us through our hospitality! Sometimes the blessing is spiritual. Other times, it is a combination of help. One weekend, my parents were staying with us, and we invited a pastor and his wife to join us for Sunday lunch. After the meal, my parents got a phone call from the police saying that their house was on fire and their teenager was having surgery in a burn unit. God used hospitality to have pastoral care in the home when the call came: our guests ended up caring for our family. It is not always that clear or particular, but fellowship with other believers almost always brings immediate blessing.

Practicing hospitality also helps bring the blessing of maturity. Self-sacrifice, service, planning, mindfulness of others, and more are all things that strip away self-centeredness, which is immaturity. Showing regular hospitality makes us regularly deny the flesh by having to clean the house when we want to read, cook when we want to check Facebook, and listen to others when we just want to talk to our spouse. The best hostesses I know are also some of the most mature Christians I know. It is not a coincidence.

It also brings the blessing of skill. Practicing hospitality is the best way to learn how to do it well. As you discover what works best for your family, how to change your routine to fit food prep, how to keep conversation going, how to fill the dishwasher while keeping a toddler happy, and so on, you will get better and better at it. The apostle tells us to "practice hospitality" because that is what all of us need—practice. Nobody is born a perfect host or hostess. We all have to learn. Consistent obedience is the best way to become skilled in opening your home and ministering to others. Talking to a skilled host or hostess helps, but nothing teaches like experience. Like any skill, good hosting can be acquired. These skills can be taught; they can be learned; they can be mastered. Let's practice!

Hospitality also brings the blessing of a stronger local church. If we are in each other's homes, tag teaming on hosting new people, reaching out to folks on the fringe, inviting strangers into God's family, *of course* we will grow closer. The strongest congregations I have been part of (nine so far, in eight different cities) have been the ones that are devoted to hospitality. People feel loved—new people and the founding members. People are working as a team—reaching out to a lost world. People are a family—occasionally fighting, but also listening, supporting, and encouraging each other. They are busy welcoming newcomers into their church family as they were welcomed into God's family. Culture does not make a difference in this equation. It does not matter if the congregation is a group of quiet highlander Scots or an outgoing, casual bunch of midwestern Americans. Congregations that do hospitality can handle external attacks, inner disagreements, and times of waiting much better than churches where folks are friendly on Sunday morning but do not open their homes to each other and strangers.

These blessings flow out of hospitality because God has wired them to do so. Obedience brings blessing, and blessings are often specific to the area of obedience. Blessings are strong encouragement to obey in the first place. And who would not want to practice hospitality when God gives results like these? It is more than worth it.

CONCLUSION

Washington Irving said, "There is an emanation from the heart in genuine hospitality, which cannot be described, but is immediately felt, and puts the stranger at once at his ease."[2] And the way to develop this emanation is to have a Christlike love for your guests. Hospitality does not come naturally to everyone; it is something that most of us need to work at, some of us more than others. It is something to pray about. It is something to practice.

As we reflect God's hospitality to us as we seek to love strangers, we can look forward to enjoying God's

---

2. Washington Irving, *The Sketch Book* (Leipzig: Bernhard Tauchnitz, 1843), 240–41.

eternal hospitality to us: endless ages as Christ's guests. Fellowship here is just a foretaste.

If you have made it this far, there is just one question left. What stranger can you invite to your home next week?

A NOTE TO MEN

Most books on hospitality seem to be directed at women. That is not all bad; we need help! But Scripture's command to practice hospitality is not merely to women. In fact, when we look at Scripture, it is almost always the men—the husbands—who are directing the hospitality. This is true from Abraham (Gen. 18:6–7) to Manoah (Judges 13:15), from Boaz (Ruth 2:14) to Gaius (Rom. 16:23). Abigail's husband, the harsh and unkind Nabal (1 Sam. 25:3), is a notable exception to men leading in this area.

And yet today in the church, we treat hospitality as though it is largely the woman's job—unless the man happens to love cooking. Perhaps part of this is because men today work outside the home full time; very few husbands are on hand to slaughter fattened calves hours before a dinner party like they were three thousand years ago. But perhaps another part of it is an unhealthy mix of unthinking abdication on the man's part and unthinking dominance on the woman's, regardless of whether she also works outside the home.

Regardless of a husband's working hours, cooking abilities, or social preferences, there are things that husbands can do to lead in showing hospitality. Just as leading the family doesn't mean that a husband does everything around the home, pays all the bills, and makes every decision, so leading in the area of hospitality does not mean that a man must arrange the schedule, draw up a menu, and leave work early to clean the bathroom—though he can! Instead, there are ways to lead his family in showing hospitality while allowing his wife to help him in this, just as Sarah helped Abraham (Gen. 18:6). Here are five.

1. Initiate hospitality. Think about people whom you should have over and ask your wife if she would be able to arrange a time for that. It can be intimidating and awkward for a wife to ask her husband if they can have people over, especially if she is not used to hosting. But she is probably the one who is reading all the good stuff on hospitality commands out there and feels as though she should do something about it—do not let her carry that burden alone. Put energy and thought into Scripture's calling in this area, then do some planning.

2. Encourage your wife. This means giving her a boost where you can—keeping the kids happy while she finishes setting the table, for example. We know a family where the husband loves to cook and often makes most of the food for guests. That is great. But encouragement will also be verbal. Few women are totally confident having people into their homes for meals, especially strangers (Heb. 3:2). Even when your wife is confident, it is still a lot of work. Tell her that you are looking forward to this visit. Let her know that you will be prepared to help during the visit, whether that means pulling up a couple more chairs from the basement or taking a screaming toddler away from the table. Tell her that she is doing a good job and that it will be a blessing to your guests. Let her know that while she is doing a lot of the work, you are doing this as a team.

3. *Lead the visit*. When your guests come, *you* lead the visit. Don't dominate it, just lead it: be at the door when the guests enter and offer to take their coats; hold the baby while your wife puts dinner on the table unless you are the one cooking. Be prepared to keep up the conversation and steer it if necessary; pray before the meal and lead in family worship when the meal is over. Do not let your wife carry the social burden, no matter how introverted you think you are.

4. *Appreciate your wife*. Let your wife know that you so appreciate her faithful work through the visit. Thank her for enabling you to obey God's command to practice hospitality. Give her a hug when the guests are gone. And if you really want to show your appreciation, help her do the dishes when everyone has left. We have had lots of quality husband-wife time debriefing over piles of dishes and then a second helping of dessert.

5. *Pray*. Thank the Lord for your guests; thank Him for the opportunity to serve in this way. Ask for

forgiveness for the ways in which you failed as a husband, father, and host during the visit. Ask God to make you more skilled in obeying this command, to better love your guests as you die to self in this area. Ask Him to send you guests and enable you to thoughtfully plan the number and frequency of hosting times. It takes wisdom to be devoted to hospitality without letting it dictate your life. And ask God to bless your hospitality for Christ's sake so that people in this broken world can see and hear of His love.